Raspberry Pi 3:
The Project Book

by
Steve McCarthy

TABLE OF CONTENTS

Introduction

This book is a guide for how to create different types of projects with the Raspberry Pi 3. It takes you through the steps to install and use OpenCV (Open Source Computer Vision Library). This is a computer vision library created to provide a uniform platform for computer applications in need of vision capabilities. You will be using this library in a number of projects. The projects in this book have mostly been using either **Python** of **Node.js** for the programming part (but you will also find a bit of **C**, and of course **Bash/Shell Script**). You are guided on how to create a surveillance camera using the Raspberry Pi. You can use it to survey your home for security purposes. The book explains how one can create a photo taker controlled by GPS. This app takes photos automatically once you reach the destinations you will personally specify. You will also come to understand how to use the Google Home and Raspberry Pi 3 together for home automation. You will also learn how to build your own Smart TV using the Raspberry Pi 3. The book helps you create an app capable of face detection using the Raspberry Pi and the Raspberry Pi camera module. You will also know how to create a print server that can be used via the network without having to migrate it from one place to another. If you don't know how to create a weather app with the Raspberry Pi, this book will help you do this.

Prerequisites

This book is a collection of practical and fun projects for the Raspberry Pi. A basic understanding of how Raspberry Pi works and how you can set it up is required to follow the contents. But don't worry if you are totally new to the world of the Pi: I have included "Chapter 0" to provide you with step-by-step instructions to set up your new microcomputer and use it for the projects discussed in the book.

If you are totally new to the Raspberry Pi, I recommend you to check out my book, *"Raspberry Pi - Essential Step by Step Beginner's Guide with Cool Projects and Programming Examples in Python,"* that covers many more basics than the introductory chapter found in this book.

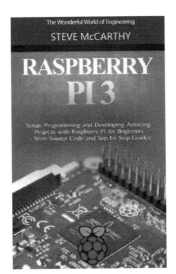

https://www.amazon.de/Raspberry-Programming-Developing-Beginners-Engineering/dp/1546685618

Chapter 0 - How to Set up the Pi

In this chapter, we will be showing you how to setup the Raspberry Pi 3 device. For the setup, you should have the following:

1. **Raspberry Pi**- make sure you have the Raspberry Pi 3 device.

2. An **HDMI monitor or television**- you will be expected to connect your Pi to a monitor, meaning that an HDMI-enabled screen will be needed.

3. A **USB mouse and keyboard**- these are paramount as they will help you control your Pi. Choose any USB mouse and keyboard.

4. A **card reader and 8GB MicroSD card**- rather than a hard drive, the operating system for the Pi should be installed on a MicroSD card. A card of a minimum of 8GB will be needed.

5. Power supply- a micro USB is usually used to power the Raspberry Pi. There are four ports on the Pi 3, so choose a power supply that can supply at least 2.5A.

Once you have all the above accessories, it will be time for you to get started setting up your Pi 3 device.

Using NOOBS to Install Raspbian OS onto an SD Card

You should first install the Raspbian OS on an SD card. This is an indication to begin downloading the operating system onto your computer, using a card reader to transfer it to an SD card.

There are two ways to achieve this. You can choose to do the installation of the Raspbian manually using external software or the command line tool. You may also choose to download and install NOOBS (New Out of Box Software). The latter is the simplest way to do it, and it's the one we will be using. Follow the steps given below:

1. Place the SD card in the computer or an SD card reader.

2. Download NOOBS. Choose the option for "offline and network install." This version will have Raspbian in the download.
   https://www.raspberrypi.org/downloads/noobs/

3. The SD card may have to be formatted to support the FAT file format. Find a tutorial to guide you as it is beyond the scope of this book.

4. Extract the contents you have downloaded in a zipped

format, then move them to an SD card. Once done, eject the SD card and plug it into your Raspberry Pi 3 device.

You will now be ready, and the rest of the work can be done on the Pi device. It is time to connect the monitor.

Connecting the Devices

It is easy to connect your devices to the Raspberry Pi 3. However, this process should be done in an orderly manner so that the Pi 3 can recognize all the devices you attach.

You should begin by connecting the HDMI cable to the Raspberry Pi 3 and the monitor, and finally adding the USB devices. For those using an Ethernet cable to establish a connection to a router, just do it.

After you have connected everything, connect the power adapter. Raspberry Pi has no power switch; it turns on automatically after you have connected it to the power supply.

Setting up the Raspbian

Once you boot up the NOOBS for the first time, it will take a few minutes to format the SD card and then setup other things, so you have to give it time. A screen will be displayed asking you to install the operating system, which can be done as follows:

1. Move to the bottom of the screen, then choose the

language you want to use as well as the keyboard layout you need based on your location.

2. Click on button next to the Raspbian, then on Install.

You should give the NOOBS time to install the Raspbian OS; it will take about 10 to 20 minutes. Once the process is complete, the system will restart and you will be taken to the desktop; and it is from here that you will be able to perform any necessary configuration. Congratulations, now you have "upgraded" your Raspberry Pi to a Raspbian Pi :-)

Configuring the Raspbian Pi

The Raspbian OS comes with a Start menu from which you can launch the file browser, open applications and everything you may need from your operating system. Begin by setting up a connection to a Wi-Fi network and any Bluetooth devices you may need.

Connecting to the Wi-Fi Network

The process of connecting a Raspbian OS is done in a similar manner as with other modern operating systems. To connect to a Wi-Fi network, follow the steps below:

1. Move to the top right corner of the screen, then click on network icon--the one with two computers.

2. Choose the name of the Wi-Fi to which you need to connect, then type in your password.

If you type the correct password, you will be connected to the Wi-Fi network directly. After setting up the Wi-Fi network, you will be able to use it from both the graphical user interface and the command line.

Connecting Bluetooth Devices

You may have Bluetooth devices such as a mouse and keyboard which you will need to connect to your Pi 3 device. In such a case, you have to pair this device with the Pi. The process is determined by the device you need to connect to your Pi, but the steps are straightforward:

1. Click on the Bluetooth icon located on upper right corner of the screen.

2. Click on "Add Device."

3. Identify the device to which you need to connect, then click on it and follow the onscreen instructions to accomplish the pairing.

You must now connect your Raspberry Pi 3 to your Bluetooth device. You can play around with it and start to do what you want.

That's it for the introduction. Now let's move on to the fun part: the projects!

Chapter 1- Installing OpenCV 3

In this chapter, we will be showing you how to install and have the OpenCV 3 running on your Raspberry Pi 3. Our assumption is that you have your Raspberry Pi 3 already installed with the Raspbian Jessie. Also, ensure that you have access to the Raspberry Pi 3 terminal, either physically or from a remote location.

For those who have ever installed OpenCV on any platform, you must be aware that there are so many dependencies and pre-requisites needed and it can be time consuming.

Let us get started with the installation process:

Expanding the Filesystem

If you have just installed the Raspbian Jessie, your first step should be to expand its filesystem so that it can occupy all the space available on the Micro-SD card. Run the following command:

```
$ sudo raspi-config
```

A new window will pop up asking you to choose an action from the available options. Choose the first option, which is "1. Expand File System" by hitting the enter key on your keyboard. Use the down arrow key to move to the <Finish>

button to reboot the Pi by running the following command:

```
$ sudo reboot
```

After the reboot, the filesystem should have been expanded to include all the space available on the Micro-SD card. To verify whether this has happened, you only have to run the "df –h" command.

A number of gigabytes are needed during the compile time for the OpenCV and its dependencies. This means that we should free up some space on the Pi by deleting the Wolfram engine. Just run the following command:

```
$ sudo apt-get purge wolfram-engine
```

Once the wolfram engine has been removed, you will have reclaimed about 700mb.

Installing the Dependencies

First, update and upgrade the already existing packages. Run the following commands:

```
$ sudo apt-get update
$ sudo apt-get upgrade
```

A number of developer tools should then be installed, including the CMake which will help in the configuration of the OpenCV build process. Run the following command:

```
$ sudo apt-get install build-essential cmake pkg-config
```

We can then install a number of image I/O packages that will make it possible to load a number of image file formats from the disk. Such file formats will include TIFF, JPEG, PNG, etc. Run the following command:

```
$ sudo apt-get install libjpeg-dev libtiff5-dev libjasper-
dev libpng12-dev
```

Video I/O packages will also be needed. Such packages will help us load video files of various formats from the disk during streaming. Install them by running the following command:

unable to locate libv4l-dev

```
$ sudo apt-get install libavcodec-dev libavformat-dev
libswscale-dev libv4l-dev
$ sudo apt-get install libxvidcore-dev libx264-dev
```

The openCV library has a module named "highgui" used for the display of images on the screen as well as for building some basic GUIs. For this module to be compiled, we should first install GTK development library as follows:

```
$ sudo apt-get install libgtk2.0-dev
```

We can optimize majority of operations inside the OpenCV by installing other dependencies. This can be done as follows:

```
$ sudo apt-get install libatlas-base-dev gfortran
```

The libraries are good for the optimization of devices that are constrained, like the Raspberry Pi.

We also need to be able to compile our OpenCV with Python bindings. This calls for us to install either Python 2.7 or Python 3 header files, as shown below:

```
$ sudo apt-get install python2.7-dev python3-dev
```

If you skip this step, you will encounter errors later on.

Downloading OpenCV Source Code

After setting everything up, we can go ahead and get the OpenCV archive from the OpenCV repository. After getting the archive, make sure you unzip it. The following commands will help you download and unzip the file:

```
$ cd ~
$ wget -O opencv.zip
https://github.com/Itseez/opencv/archive/3.1.0.zip
$ unzip opencv.zip
```

Our aim is to have full installation of the OpenCV 3, which means that we should also get the opencv-contrib as shown below:

```
$ wget -O opencv_contrib.zip
https://github.com/Itseez/opencv_contrib/archive/3.1.0.zip
$ unzip opencv_contrib.zip
```

Note that it is good for you to ensure you get the same versions for the OpenCV and opencv-contrib. If you fail to ensure this, you will get an error during the compile or run time.

Before we can compile the OpenCV just downloaded, we should first install "pip", a Python package manager. This can be done as follows:

```
$ wget https://bootstrap.pypa.io/get-pip.py
$ sudo python get-pip.py
```

If you need to keep the various dependencies in separate places, you can use the concept of virtual environment. You can achieve this by installing the following two packages:

```
$ sudo pip install virtualenv virtualenvwrapper
$ sudo rm -rf ~/.cache/pip
```

Now that you have installed the above two packages, you should update the "~/.profile" file to include the lines given below at the bottom:

```
# virtualenv and virtualenvwrapper
export WORKON_HOME=$HOME/.virtualenvs
source /usr/local/bin/virtualenvwrapper.sh
```

Note that you can use any text editor of choice to do the above. Examples of such editors include the nano, vim and emacs. Now that you have made changes to the file, you should restart the machine for them to take effect. Also, you can close the current terminal instance and launch another one, or joust logout then log into the system again. You can also achieve this by running the following command:

```
$ source ~/.profile
```

Creating a Virtual Environment for Python

This is the environment that will be used for the computer vision development. Run the following command:

```
$ mkvirtualenv cv -p python2
```

The above command is for users of Python 2.7, and it will help you create a virtual Python environment named "cv". For the users of Python 3, the following command will help you achieve the same:

```
$ mkvirtualenv cv -p python3
```

Thw workon command will then take you to the virtual environment:

```
$ source ~/.profile
$ workon cv
```

To perform a validation and be sure that you are in the cv virtual environment, you will examine the command line; if you see the word "cv" preceding the prompt, then you know that you are in the cv virtual environment. Otherwise, you will not be in the cv virtual environment. To solve this, you will have to run the workon and source commands.

Installing NumPy

You should now be in the cv virtual environment. NumPy is the only package in this case, and it is highly used for numerical processing. Run the following command to install the package:

```
$ pip install numpy
```

Installation will take around 10 minutes.

8:56:40 — 9:08:14
11:34
mm:ss

Compiling and Installing OpenCV

It is now the right time to compile and install the OpenCV. Ensure that you are in the cv virtual environment by double checking the command line. To move to the cv virtual environment, just run the "workon" command as shown below:

✓

```
$ workon cv
```

After you are sure that you are in the cv virtual environment, you can go ahead and make the build by use of CMake as

14

shown below:

```
$ cd ~/opencv-3.1.0/
$ mkdir build
$ cd build
$ cmake -D CMAKE_BUILD_TYPE=RELEASE \
    -D CMAKE_INSTALL_PREFIX=/usr/local \
    -D INSTALL_PYTHON_EXAMPLES=ON \
    -D OPENCV_EXTRA_MODULES_PATH=~/opencv_contrib-
3.1.0/modules \
    -D BUILD_EXAMPLES=ON ..
```

Have a look at the output given above before we can proceed to the compilation step. You can scroll to the section showing the Python version you are using, either Python 2.7 or Python 3, and ensure that valid paths to the libraries, numPy, interpreter and packages have been set properly.

After this, you will be ready to compile the OpenCV. Run the following command: *it looks like it built on Py2.7*

```
$ make -j4
```

The use of the –j4 command helps control the number of cores which will be leveraged during the compilation of OpenCV 3. Note that we have used a value of 4 because the Raspberry Pi 2 has 4 cores, which will make it compile faster.

However, errors may occur during the compilation due to the use of the many cores. In such a case, it will be good for you to begin the compilation process and use only one core.

```
$ make clean
$ make
```

Prior to this step:

(cv) pi@ Off-Network: ~/opencv-3.1.0/build $

After a successful compilation, proceed to the next step and install the OpenCV 3 by running the following commands;

```
$ sudo make install
$ sudo ldconfig
```

If you are using Python 2.7 and the OpenCV 3 has installed with no error, the installation should have been done in /usr/local/lib/python2.7/site-packages.
To finish the installation, we should sym-link the bindings of the OpenCV into the cv virtual environment for Python 2.7. The following commands will help achieve this:

```
$ cd ~/.virtualenvs/cv/lib/python2.7/site-packages/
$ ln -s /usr/local/lib/python2.7/site-packages/cv2.so cv2.so
```

In Python 3, the installation of the OpenCV and the Python bindings should be done in /usr/local/lib/python3.4/site-packages. The sym-link can then be done by running the following commands:

```
$ cd ~/.virtualenvs/cv/lib/python3.4/site-packages/
$ ln -s /usr/local/lib/python3.4/site-packages/cv2.so cv2.so
```

At this point, the installation should be done. To test whether everything has run successfully, open a new terminal, run the "workon" and "source" commands, then import Python + OpenCV bindings as shown below:

.

```
$ source ~/.profile
$ workon cv
$ python
>>> import cv2
>>> cv2.__version__
'3.1.0'
>>>
```

The OpenCV version should show if the installation is successful.

Chapter 2- Building a Surveillance Camera with the Pi

In this chapter, we will be guiding you how to build a surveillance camera from the Raspberry Pi. The Pi will be recording a HD video once something moves in the area being monitoring. The owner will be able to view a live video on their browser, even with the use of mobile when on the road.

Assemble the following hardware components:

1. Raspberry Pi 3 Model B.

2. Raspberry Pi camera module. It comes with a connector that can be connected to the board.

3. A housing for your camera.

4. Power supply for the Raspberry Pi.

5. SD card.

6. A network connection that will help you connect your Pi to a network.

First, if you don't have the OS installed on your Raspberry Pi, begin by installing it. After the installation, ensure that it is up to date by running the following commands:

```
sudo apt-get install rpi-update
```

```
sudo rpi-update
```

Also, make sure that the packages are updated by running the following commands:

```
sudo apt-get update
sudo apt-get upgrade
```

Establishing a Remote Connection

Now that everything has been setup on your Pi, you should connect to it from your computer. Users of the Windows operating system will have to download and install PuTTy on their computers, which will help them connect to the Linux terminal on the Pi. After that, you will not need a monitor or keyboard connected to the Pi device.

Enable Wi-Fi

If you are in need of running a camera by use of a Wi-Fi USB dongle, an additional step will be needed to make the Wi-Fi work on the Pi.
Open the PuTTy on your Windows and then open the network configuration file by running the following command:

```
sudo nano /etc/network/interfaces
```

The file will be opened in the nano editor. Add the lines given below at the bottom of the file.

```
allow-hotplug wlan0
iface wlan0 inet dhcp
wpa-ssid "YOUR NETWORK SSID"
wpa-psk "WIFI PASSWORD"
```

Ensure that you replace the details given above with the SSID and password for the network. Run the following command to reboot the Pi and check whether it is connecting correctly to the network:

```
sudo reboot
```

Assembling the Hardware

It is now time for us to assemble all the hardware components together. This will be determined by the housing you are using. Your camera LED will light up red each time motion is recorded. If you need to turn off this LED, you can add the line below to the /boot/config.txt file:

```
disable_camera_led=1
```

Installation of Motion Detection Software

"Motion" is a good motion detection or surveillance software as it provides multiple configuration options. This software

can be installed from the command line by running the
following:

```
sudo apt-get install motion
```

A number of packages will be installed during the installation
process, so you just have to type "y' for the installation to
continue. The available version of the motion software does
not have support for the camera module of the Raspberry Pi.
This calls for us to download then install a special build will
help us use the Raspberry Pi camera module. The following
commands will help achieve this:

```
cd /tmp
sudo apt-get install -y libjpeg62 libjpeg62-dev
libavformat53 libavformat-dev libavcodec53 libavcodec-dev
libavutil51 libavutil-dev libc6-dev zlib1g-dev
libmysqlclient18 libmysqlclient-dev libpq5 libpq-dev
wget https://www.dropbox.com/s/xdfcxm5hu71s97d/motion-
mmal.tar.gz
```

The downloaded file should then be unpacked to the /tmp
directory:

```
tar zxvf motion-mmal.tar.gz
```

You can then use the downloaded build to update the
downloaded motion. The following commands will help you
achieve this:

```
sudo mv motion /usr/bin/motion
sudo mv motion-mmalcam.conf /etc/motion.conf
```

The motion daemon should also be enabled for motion to execute always:

```
sudo nano /etc/default/motion
```

The above command will open its configuration file in the nano editor. You can then change the line to the following:

```
start_motion_daemon=yes
```

The official build of the motion software is capable of supporting the Raspberry camera module. If you need to edit the configuration file for the software, run the following command:

```
sudo nano /etc/motion.conf
```

It is your duty to ensure that the right permissions are set. If the motion is installed via SSH by a user logged in as "pi", it will be good for you to give the user named "motion" permission to execute the motion software as a service after a reboot. This can be done as follows:

```
sudo chmod 664 /etc/motion.conf
sudo chmod 755 /usr/bin/motion
sudo touch /tmp/motion.log
sudo chmod 775 /tmp/motion.log
```

You should also ensure that the motion is running in the background in the form of a daemon. Our aim is to store the log file in /tmp. We have to run the following command:

```
logfile /tmp/motion.log
```

We also need to use some high-quality surveillance video. This is why the resolution has been set to 1280x720 as shown below:

```
width 1280
height 720
```

A real time video is not of importance in this case, but 2 pictures per second will be enough for us:

```
framerate 2
```

We need to configure the motion software to record some frames before and after motion in the image is detected. These have been set to 2 in our configuration:

```
pre_capture 2
post_capture 2
```

We need each motion video to take a maximum of 10 minutes only. This can be configured by use of the "max_mpeg_time" configuration option. This option will work well with the motion-mmal build, but in case you get the error "Unknown config option 'max_mpeg_time'", you will have to use the max_movie_time or the motion-mmal build.

```
max_mpeg_time 600
```

A number of video players such as VLC will not be able to play the videos recorded, which is why we have changed the codec to msmpeg4. After that, the movies will play well in all players:

```
ffmpeg_video_codec msmpeg4
```

We also need to access the live stream from anywhere. If we fail to configure this, then only the local host will be able to access the live stream. The following command will help us enable this:

```
stream_localhost off
```

If you are in need of protecting the live stream by use of a username and a password, then you only have to enable the following:

```
stream_auth_method 2
stream_authentication SOMEUSERNAME:SOMEPASSWORD
```

Once the above changes have been made to the motion.conf file, you can reboot the Pi:

```
sudo reboot
```

After the reboot, you will see the red light of your camera go on, which is an indication that the motion is using your camera for motion detection.

Saving the Videos

The SD card of Raspberry Pi has limited space. This is why we will be storing the recorded videos on a Window server.
Begin by sharing a folder or folders from a windows machine. Whether you are accessing the Pi from PuTTy or directly launch the fstab configuration on the Raspberry, execute:

```
sudo nano /etc/fstab
```

An extra line showing the configuration of the Windows network shared folder should be added:

//YOURSERVERNAME/YOURSHAREDFOLDERNAME /mnt/camshare   cifs username=YOURSHAREDFOLDERUSERNAME,password= YOURSHAREDFOLDERPASSWORD,iocharset=utf8,file_m ode=0777,dir_mode=0777 0 0

Be sure that the user has been granted permissions to save files to your shared folder. After rebooting the Pi, it should have the folder /mnt/Camshare mounted to your Windows shared folder. You can then set this in a motion.cofig file as shown below:

target_dir /mnt/camshare

After this, motion will be saving all the videos in the shared folder of your Windows machine.

Fix Motion Autostart

You may experience a problem as the motion may not be started automatically once the Pi is rebooted. The reason is because the mounted folder on Windows is not ready when motion is trying to access it. To solve this, open the following file:

sudo nano /etc/init.d/motion

Then edit it by adding the following line to start a sequence:

sleep 30

Mounting the Camera

At this point, the surveillance camera can be mounted to destination point. You can now use any browser to access the live stream from the camera using the URL http://IPADDRESSOFRASPBERRY:8080. You can check for the port you are using on your system from the motion.conf file, then use it to replace the port 8080.

If you need to access the live stream from any location, then you will have to enable some dynamic domain services to the local network. With this, you will be able to connect to the local IP address from outside even after changes to the local

IP address. A good example of a service that can help you achieve this is dyn.com. After setting up the dynamic IP url, you will be in a position to access the camera stream from your browser despite your location. This also applies to you if you are using a mobile device.

There are multiple things you can do by use of the surveillance camera. You may make it send notifications once some motion has been detected. A temperature sensor can also be added. A battery pack can be added to the camera if there is a need for extra security. You should ensure that you buy one capable of charging while powering the Pi device at the same time.

Chapter 3- GPS Controlled Photo Taker

Whenever you are travelling, you will want to take pictures. However, some people hate to stop for this purpose. An automated photo take can help.

In this chapter, we will create an automated photo taker controlled by GPS. You will pre-select the places at which you need to take photos, and the app will automatically take them once you get near the place.

Requirements

- Raspberry Pi 3 Model B

- GPS Module U-blox NEO-6M with a 3m Active Antenna (STM32 51)

- PNY 7800 PowerPack

- GoPro HERO Series Camera

- GoPro 3-Way

You should hook a GPS module to the Raspberry Pi which will send a signal to GoPro through Wi-Fi. No soldering is needed; you just have to use a USB to plug the GPS module to your Raspberry Pi. You will use the Wi-Fi from the GoPro in the Raspberry Pi. The GoPro app can be used for configuring the SSD of the Wi-Fi. The Pi should be powered from a battery pack.

You should determine the coordinates for all the places at which you need to take photos. We will then write a Python script to help us calculate or determine the distance between the coordinates. Note that this script will start running immediately when the Raspberry Pi is turned on so as to check the coordinates.

You can use the GoPro API Library to establish a connection from the GoPro to the Raspberry Pi via Wi-Fi. The library can be installed by use of pip as shown below:

```
pip install goprocam
```

Note: in my case, I am in London, so I calculate the coordinates for the places I need to take photos in the city. I have written a Python script for this job. The script has an initialization of the camera as shown below:

```
camera = GoProCamera.GoPro()
```

The following line will then help us take the pictures:

```
camera.take_photo(0)
```

In this case, 0 refers to the time it will wait before taking the picture.

The gpsd-py3 should be installed. In my case, I have used pip. The following command will help you install this:

```
$ pip3 install gpsd-py3
```

The GPS daemon can then be pointed to GPS device. The line given below should be added to the "/etc/rc.local" file:

```
gpsd /dev/ttyACM0 -F /var/run/gpsd.sock
```

Our aim is to have our script executed once the Raspberry Pi is started. On the same file, that is, /etc/rc.local, add the following line:

```
python3 /home/pi/PictureScript.py
```

Note that "PictureScript.py" is the name of the script responsible for calculating the distance between the various London coordinates. Now that we have added it to the above file, it will be executed each time the Raspberry Pi is started.

PicturesScript.py

The calculations will done in this script. It will run on startup, then poll to check your coordinates against some list of coordinates you have select. The code for the script is as follows:

```python
import time
import gpsd
import math
from goprocam import GoProCamera
from goprocam import constants

#for calculating your current location
earthRadius = 6371

#Wait for Pi to boot then get the GoPro Wifi
time.sleep(20)

gpsd.connect()

camera = GoProCamera.GoPro()

#Saved Locations for the trip:
#Platform 9 3/4: 51.5322° , -0.1240°
#Abbey Road: 51.5321° , -0.1781°
#Buckingham 51.5014°, -0.1419°
#Big Ben 51.5007° , -0.1246°
#Tower of London 51.5081° , -0.0759°
#Tower Bridge 51.5055° , -0.0754°
#Shakespeare Globe 51.5081° , -0.0972°
#Sweetings 51.5125° , -0.0928°

#Create location arrays:
latitude = [51.5110, 51.5322, 51.5321, 51.5014, 51.5007, 51.5081, 51.5055,
51.5081, 51.5125]
longitude = [-0.1863, -0.1240, -0.1781, -0.1419, -0.1246, -0.0759, -0.0754, -
0.0972, -0.0928]

while True:
    received = False
    try:
        packet = gpsd.get_current()
        received = True
    except Exception:
        print("No signal")

    if received == True:
        #get my current position
        currentPost = packet.position()
        currentLat = currentPost[0]
        currentLon = currentPost[1]
        for location in range(len(latitude)):
            dLat = math.radians(latitude[location] - currentLat)
            dLon = math.radians(longitude[location] - currentLon)

            # a = sin²(Δφ/2) + cos φ1 · cos φ2 · sin²(Δλ/2)
            # c = 2 · atan2( √a, √(1-a) )
            #d = R · c
            a = math.sin(dLat/2) * math.sin(dLat/2) \
              + math.cos(math.radians(latitude[location])) \
              * math.cos(math.radians(currentLat)) * math.sin(dLon/2) \
              * math.sin(dLon/2)
            c = 2 * math.atan2(math.sqrt(a), math.sqrt(1-a))
            d = earthRadius * c

            if d < 0.01:
                camera.take_photo(0)

    time.sleep(1)
```

Note that we began by importing all the libraries needed with the use of the "import" keyword. A connection has then been established to the local gpsd in the line "gpsd.connect()". The line "camera = GoProCamera.GoPro()" helps us initialize the camera object. The locations have been stored in an array. The "while" loop helps us check the current coordinates we are at as well as the coordinates that have been saved.

We have used the haversine formula to calculate the distance between the coordinates. The variable "d" has been used to represent the distance between two coordinates. A picture will only be taken if d is found to be less than 10m, which is equivalent to 0.01km.

Chapter 4- Google Assistant in Raspberry Pi

In this project, we will be adding an indicator similar to that of Google Home for the Google Assistant running on the Raspberry Pi. The following components have been used in the project:

- Raspberry Pi 3 Model B

- Google AIY Projects Kit

- Microphone

- Speakers

- Adafruit NeoPixel Ring: WS2812 5050 RGB LED

- Jumper wires (generic)

- Everything ESP Wemos D1 Mini

- Arduino IDE

- Google Assistant SDK

After assembling all the above components, connect the Wemos D1 Mini and the Raspberry Pi as shown below:

The pins can be changed depending on the board you are using and the neopixel ring. After that, upload the following code to your Arduino software:

```
#include <Adafruit_NeoPixel.h>

int numPixels = 12;
#define BUTTON_PIN1    D2
#define BUTTON_PIN2    D3
Adafruit_NeoPixel strip =
Adafruit_NeoPixel(numPixels, neoPixelPin, NEO_GRB +
NEO_KHZ800);

int start1 = 0;
int start2 = 3;
int start3 = 6;
int start4 = 9;
int brightness = 150;
```

```
int brightDirection = -15;
#define DELAY_TIME (50)
unsigned long startTime;

void setup() {
  pinMode(BUTTON_PIN1, INPUT);
  pinMode(BUTTON_PIN2, INPUT);
  strip.begin();
  strip.show();
  startTime = millis();
  activatecircle();
  activateblink();
}

void loop() {
  bool but1 = digitalRead(BUTTON_PIN1);
  bool but2 = digitalRead(BUTTON_PIN2);
  if (but1 == HIGH) {
    delay(10);
    if ( startTime + DELAY_TIME < millis() ) {
      activateblink();
      startTime = millis();
    }
  }
  else if (but2 == HIGH) {
    delay(10);
    if ( startTime + DELAY_TIME < millis() ) {
      activatecircle();
      startTime = millis();
    }
  }
  else {
    allOff();
  }
}
```

```
void allOff() {
  for ( int i = 0; i < numPixels; i++ ) {
    strip.setPixelColor(i, 0, 0, 0 );
  }
  strip.show();
}

void activatecircle() {
  adjustStarts();
  for ( int i = start1; i < start1 + 1; i++ ) {
    strip.setPixelColor(i, 23, 107, 239 );
  }
  for ( int i = start2; i < start2 + 1 ; i++ ) {
    strip.setPixelColor(i, 255, 62, 48 );
  }
  for ( int i = start3; i < start3 + 1; i++ ) {
    strip.setPixelColor(i, 247, 181, 41 );
  }
  for ( int i = start4; i < start4 + 1; i++ ) {
    strip.setPixelColor(i, 23, 156, 82 );
  }
  strip.show();
}

void activateblink() {
  for ( int i = start1; i < start1 + 1; i++ ) {
    strip.setPixelColor(i, 23, 107, 239 );
    strip.setBrightness(brightness);
    strip.show();
    adjustBrightness();
  }
  for ( int i = start2; i < start2 + 1 ; i++ ) {
    strip.setPixelColor(i, 255, 62, 48 );
    strip.setBrightness(brightness);
```

```
      strip.show();
      adjustBrightness();
   }
   for ( int i = start3; i < start3 + 1; i++ ) {
      strip.setPixelColor(i, 247, 181, 41 );
      strip.setBrightness(brightness);
      strip.show();
      adjustBrightness();
   }
   for ( int i = start4; i < start4 + 1; i++ ) {
      strip.setPixelColor(i, 23, 156, 82 );
      strip.setBrightness(brightness);
      strip.show();
    adjustBrightness();
   }
   strip.show();
}

void adjustStarts() {
   start1 = incrementStart(start1);
   start2 = incrementStart(start2);
   start3 = incrementStart(start3);
   start4 = incrementStart(start4);
}

int incrementStart(int startValue) {
   startValue = startValue + 1;
   if ( startValue == 12 )
      startValue = 0;
   return startValue;
}

void adjustBrightness() {
   brightness = brightness + brightDirection;
   if ( brightness < 0 ) {
```

```
    brightness = 0;
    brightDirection = -brightDirection;
  }
  else if ( brightness > 255 ) {
    brightness = 255;
    brightDirection = -brightDirection;
  }

  Serial.println( brightness );
}
```

Note that you can change the pin numbers depending on the board you are using. We have also defined 4 pixels, each representing a Google color. The "for" loop helps us set different colors for the pixels in intervals of 20.

Chapter 5- Raspberry Pi 3 Gaming

To be able to stream Steam to your Raspberry Pi, you should have the following components:

- Raspberry Pi 3

- Steam installed with steam games

- 5V 2.5A Power Supply

- Xbox 360 Wired Controller

- 8GB+ Micro SD card

- A Windows PC with GTX650+ NVidia Graphics Card

A 2.5A power supply should be used to power the Raspberry Pi. Samsung SD Cards are the best, as they support the Wire Laveling technology which makes the card serve for a longer time. Your computer should be installed with Windows 7, 8, 8.1 or 10.

Ensure that your Raspberry Pi 3 is installed with the latest version of Raspbian OS.

Next, install Moonlight into the Raspberry Pi 3. The Raspbian command line will be needed for this task.

Let us add the source from which we will download Moonlight by running the following command:

```
sudo bash -c 'printf "deb
http://archive.itimmer.nl/raspbian/moonlight jessie
main\n" >> /etc/apt/sources.list'
```

We can then update the system and install the Moonlight by running the following two commands:

```
sudo apt-get update
```

```
sudo apt-get install moonlight-embedded
```

You will then have Moonlight installed in your Raspberry Pi.

Discovering the Computer's IP Address

You should discover the IP address of the machine having the Steam installed on it. To do this, press the Windows key on your computer, begin to type CMD, then hit the enter key. A command prompt will be started, so type the following command on it:

```
ipconfig
```

You will then be able to determine the IP address of your computer. Once you have obtained it, you can go back to setting up Moonlight.

Configuring Moonlight

It is time to pair the Raspberry Pi with Gamestream service in the GeForce Experience. You just have to run the following command in the command prompt of the Pi, with the 192.168... being the IP address of your computer:

```
moonlight pair 192.168…
```

Note the PIN number generated by the Raspberry Pi, then go back to your computer installed with Steam.
The GeForce should now pop up some window which will prompt the PIN to be entered. Type the PIN, then click CONNECT. You should now see your Raspberry Pi display "paired".

Starting Moonlight

Now that you have paired up everything, you should connect the Xbox 360 controller, then run the following command on the Raspberry Pi 3's command prompt to start Moonlight:

```
moonlight stream -1080 -30fps -app Steam
```

It is possible for you to change a number of settings such as the -720 instead of -1080, and -60fps instead of the -30fps if you need to increase the frames. You will then be done!

Chapter 6- Creating a Node.JS Web Server

In this chapter, we will be building a Node.js server on the Raspberry Pi 3. You will also familiarize yourself with resin.io basics. You will know how to get the Raspberry Pi 3 online and then upload some Node.js code to it.

Begin by assembling the following components:

- A Raspberry Pi 3 Model B
- A 4GB or a larger microSD card
- An ethernet cable (optional)
- A micro USB cable
- A 2A USB micro power supply (optional)
- A resin.io account

If you have not created a resin.io account, just open its home page and begin to sign up. You will be asked to set up some SSH key so that you can push the code securely.

SSH keys use the concept of public key cryptography so that the connection can be secured when you are sending your code. For your Git connection to remain secured, you should add a public SSH key.

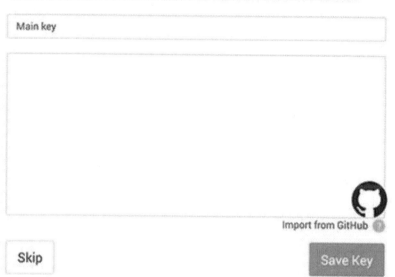

Enter your SSH Key

We need your public SSH key to authenticate you when you push changes to your application's git repo. Don't know what this is? Check out GitHub's instructions.

Main key

Import from GitHub

Skip

Save Key

Paste the public key into the provided box, then click "Save Key". If you need to import the key from Github, just click the Octocat icon.

Creating the Application

To create the application, type the name for the application, choose the Raspberry Pi 3 from the drop down, then click on the create button. You will be taken to the dashboard for your app.

Adding the First Device

All the devices that have been connected to your application should be shown on the dashboard, together with their logs and statuses.

Click on "Download resinOS" to begin downloading the resin.io operating system image for the application. A drop down will be shown with a list of all available versions. Choose the latest.

A prompt will appear asking you to specify the means of connecting the device to the Internet. You can use either an Ethernet cable or Wi-Fi. For the former, you don't need to do any configuration; but for the latter, you will have to configure the network SSID and the passphrase.

Once you have chosen the connectivity option, click on "Download Device OS" and the resion.io OS will be downloaded together with the necessary settings for the network and the application. After the download is complete, you will get a file with an .img extension, which is the image.

Creating a Bootable SD Card

It is now time to send the .img file to the SD card. Etcher is the best tool for this purpose, as it will help you write the image to the SD card and validate it. Install it now!

You can also use other SD card writers such as win32diskimager.

Once the Etcher has been installed, just start it. The following steps will help you create a bootable SD card with the resinOS:

1. Click on "Select image" button, then find the resinOS `.img` file for your applications.
2. If you have not already done this, insert the SD card into the computer. Etcher will detect it automatically. If you have inserted more than one SD card, you will have to select the right one.
3. Click on "Flash!" button.

The Etcher will create a bootable SD card for you and perform a validation as to whether it was done correctly. Once the process is complete, the SD card will be ejected.

Device Setup

Insert the SD card into your Raspberry Pi 3, then establish a connection to the Internet. Insert the Micro USB cable to power the Raspberry Pi 3.

It will take about 3 minutes to see the Raspberry Pi 3 on the resin.io dashboard. As you wait for the partitions on the SD card to be expanded, install a custom Linux environment, then establish a secure connection with the servers.

Deploying the Code

Since we have connected one or two devices to the resin.io application, we can go ahead and deploy some code and then begin to build something.

You can begin by creating an Express.js web server to serve a static page on the port :80. Here is the code for the server.js:

```
var express = require('express');
var app = express();

// reply to request with "Hello World!"
app.get('/', function (req, res) {
  res.send('Hello World!');
});

//start a server on port 80 and log its start to our
console
var server = app.listen(80, function () {
  var port = server.address().port;
  console.log('Example app listening on port ', port);
});
```

Since the project can be accessed on Github, we can clone it by running the following command:

```
$ git clone https://github.com/resin-io-
projects/simple-server-node.git
```

After the repository has been cloned, you can change your directory to the one newly created, the simple-server-node directory, then run the following command to add resin git remote endpoint:

```
$ cd simple-server-node
$ git remote add resin
<USERNAME>@git.resin.io:<USERNAME>/<APPNAME>.git
```

We will have set a reference in the local Git repository to the resin.io application remote repository. After pushing to the remote repository, it will be compiled, then be built on the servers, then deployed to each device in our application fleet. The following command will help deploy the code to all devices contained in the application:

```
$ git push resin master
```

To replace the source code of your application with some new source tree, you can run the "`git push resin master -force`" command so as to force the push.

If you see the friendly unicorn mascot in the terminal, know that the compilation was successful. This code should now be stored in the image registry.

All devices connected to the application fleet will download and execute the application.

At this point, you should have a Node.js web server running on the device and see logs on the dashboard. If you open the "Actions" page for the device, enable the public URL and it will be accessible from any place in the world. If you follow the URL, you will get a page with "Hello, World!" text. You can also point the browser to the IP address of your machine.

The root directory of our project will have a number of files including Dockerfile.template, package.json and server.js. The .template file will allow you to define the variables for the template like "%%RESIN_MACHINE_NAME%%" which will help you to push a repository to multiple and different architecture fleets.

Below is the first line of the Dockerfile.template file:

```
FROM resin/%%RESIN_MACHINE_NAME%%-node:slim
```

The placeholder "%%RESIN_MACHINE_NAME%%" will be replaced with the name of the resin device. Since you are using a Raspberry Pi 3, this line will be as follows:

```
FROM resin/raspberrypi3-node:slim
```

This tells the resin builder that we need to use this image as the base. There is a ":slim" tag associated with the base image denoting what the stripped-down version to have minimal packages needs to run the node, meaning that there will be no node-gyp as well as other build essentials.
The following lines have been commented out:

RUN apt-get update && apt-get install -yq \
  alsa-utils libasound2-dev && \
  apt-get clean && rm -rf /var/lib/apt/lists/*

This demonstrates how the apt-get can be used for installation of dependencies in a container. We will be installing some useful Linux sound utilities. The whole code for the .template file should be as follows:
FROM resin/%%RESIN_MACHINE_NAME%%-node:slim

WORKDIR /usr/src/app

COPY package.json package.json

48

RUN JOBS=MAX npm install --production --unsafe-perm && npm cache clean && rm -rf /tmp/*

COPY . ./

ENV INITSYSTEM on

CMD ["npm", "start"]

The WORDIR helps us set the working directory for COPY, RUN and CMD commands which follow it.

We can now go ahead and build the node.js dependencies and modules using the RUN command. We have also used the – production flag to build and clear the cache to keep our final image smaller.

After the npm install, the rest of the code will be copied to the working directory, and this is done later so that the builds can benefit from the build caching. A full npm install will only be triggered once something in the package.json file is changed. Below is the code for package.json file:

```
{
  "name": "simple-server-node",
  "version": "1.0.0",
  "description": "A simple Expressjs Web server on
resin.io",
  "main": "server.js",
  "scripts": {
    "test": "echo \"Error: no test specified\" && exit 1",
    "start": "node server.js"
  },
```

```
"repository": {
  "type": "git",
  "url": "git+https://github.com/resin-io-
projects/simple-server-node.git"
},
"keywords": [
  "resin.io",
  "webserver",
  "nodejs",
  "expressjs"
],
"author": "Stefan <stefan@resin.io>",
"license": "Apache-2.0",
"bugs": {
  "url": "https://github.com/resin-io-projects/simple-
server-node/issues"
},
"homepage": "https://github.com/resin-io-projects/simple-
server-node#readme",
"dependencies": {
  "express": "*"
}
}
```

In the section for dependencies, we have defined the node modules and the versions we need to use in the application. The scripts allow us point to the server.js as the starting point for whole application.

Web Terminal

This is built on the dashboard and helps in running commands and checking log files. To start it on your device, the following are expected:

1. An online device
2. A running container

Number 1 is easy, but number 2 is somehow hard. If the docker's main process crashes or ends, the container will stop and your web terminal will have nothing to which to SSH. To ensure that the container is always up and running during development, use the system init system.

To launch a session, navigate to >_Terminal page for your device then hit the button for "Start the terminal session". Some seconds will elapse before a new session can be established and you will be ready to go.

Resin Sync for Faster Development

At this point, you are aware how to provision a device, then push code. The resin sync command line tool will allow you to sync your source code quickly, then file the changes across the devices in the fleet.

Setting up the Resin Sync

The Resin sync comes with the resin CLI. It will allow you to do all the tasks from the command line.

For you to install the resin CLI and sync, your machine should be installed with node.js 4.0.0 and above. The following command will help you install resin:

```
$ npm install --global --production resin-cli
```

You must have administrative privileges to be able to run the above command. Once the CLI has been installed, use your resin account to login:

```
$ resin login
```

You will be prompted to choose the best login method, with the best being web authorization. This method will present a dialog in your browser, and you will be asked to authorize the use of the CLI.

Set Up Node.js Cross-Compilation

There is no need for cross-compilation when using resin sync and the Node.js because it's an interpreted language. Begin by launching the terminal in our previous directory to begin using the resin sync.
Make some trivial change to the source code, then run the following command:

```
$ resin sync --source . --destination /usr/src/app
```

You will be prompted to choose a device, and all the files in the root of the directory will be synced to /usr/src/app on the chosen device and the container will be restarted. You will get an output related to the one given below:

```
resin:simple-server-node shaun$ resin sync --source .
--destination /usr/src/app
Getting information for device:
5dc2c87ea2caf79bc4e25ae638c6d5a35a75cecf22e8f914331dc
b2f588f4b
Application container stopped.
Synced /usr/src/app on 5dc2c87.
Application container started.

resin sync completed successfully!
```

After about 30 seconds, the new code will be up and running. The resin SSH is one of the most useful features of the resin-cli. It will allow you to perform a quick SSH into the container which is running the device, then pull out logs or run some test commands.

With the device online and having logged into the CLI, you are able to access the container by use of "resin ssh <uuid>". The following example demonstrates this:

```
resin:simple-server-node nicohsam$ resin ssh 5dc2c87
Connecting with: 5dc2c87
root@raspberrypi3-5dc2c8:/# uname -a
Linux Raspberry Pi 3-5dc2c8 3.10.93 #1 SMP PREEMPT
Wed June 14 11:25:12 CEST 2017 armv7l GNU/Linux
```

The resin.io also has many other features of which you can take advantage.

Chapter 7- Building a Smart TV

In this chapter, we will show you how to build a Smart TV with Raspberry Pi 3, Node.JS and Socket.io. Begin by assembling the following components:

- The Raspberry Pi 33 Model B
- A USB WiFi dongle or an Ethernet cable
- 8 GB+SD/MicroSD card
- Raspbian, that is, a fork of Debian developed for Raspberry Pi
- Node.js:
  - Socket.io for handling the connection between the remote and the TV via websockets
  - Express for handling basic http requests
  - Omxcontrol for some simple module for controlling the OMXPlayer
- OMXPlayer
- Youtube-dl, which is a script to allow us download YouTube videos
- Chromium Browser
- Quo.js for handling swipe gestures on mobile web app
- YouTube API
- HTML5, JavaScript, CSS3 transitions, and Moustache in the form of a template engine

The first step should be to install the Raspbian and the Node. js in your Raspberry Pi. My assumption is that you are aware of how to install them, so we will not discuss it.

Installation of Chromium and YouTube-dl

You can use apt-get or build the chromium browser from the source. Use the following command:

```
sudo apt-get install chromium-browser
```

If you need to have a better display, install the MC core fonts by running the following command:

```
sudo apt-get install ttf-mscorefonts-installer
```

You can then run the following commands to install and then update the Youtube-dl script:

```
sudo apt-get install youtube-dl
```

```
sudo youtube-dl -U
```

The Chromium is not hardware accelerated, and it will be a bad idea for us to stream idea to the browser. The Youtube-dl is the best alternative; the video will be downloaded and streamed in the OMX-player, this being hardware accelerated in the Pi.

Note that the OMX-player comes installed in the Raspian OS.

Basic Shellcode

If you need to establish a connection to the Raspberry Pi via SSH, you should first update the DISPLAY environment variables by use of the following command:

```
export DISPLAY=:0.0
```

The graphical output you get from the session will point to the first display which has been connected to Raspberry Pi. The following command will help you check all available environment variables:

```
env
```

You can now test the Chromium while in the Kiosk mode:

```
chromium --kiosk http://www.google.com
```

The Youtube-dl can be tested as follows:

```
youtube-dl youtube_video_url
```

You can modify the Youtube-dl command by adding the following options:

```
youtube-dl  -o "%(id)s.%(ext)s" -f /22/18
youtube_video_url
```

Once you have downloaded the video, you can attempt to play it by use of the OMX-Player as shown below:

```
omxplayer youtube_video_file
```

Server-Side Scripting

The project file hierarchy should be as follows:

- public

    - js
    - css
    - images
    - fonts
    - index.html
    - remote.html

- app.js
- package.json

The file Package.json will be needed by the npm for auto-installation of dependencies and storage of the other metadata about the project. This should be as follows:

```
{
    "name": "RasPi.TV",
    "version": "0.0.1",
    "private": false,
    "scripts": {
        "start": "node app.js"
    },
    "dependencies": {
    "express": "3.1.1",
```

```
    "socket.io":"0.9.14",
    "omxcontrol":"*"
    }
}
```

You can install the dependencies by running the following command on the terminal:

```
npm install
```

A node with the name "node-modules" will be created in the project directory. If you would like to use git, create a .gitignore file and add the line "node_modules" to the file, which will help you ignore the node_modules folder from being added to the git project.

Create the file app.js then begin to create the basic HTTP server with the Express.js:

```
var express = require('express')
  , app = express()
  , server = require('http').createServer(app)
  , path = require('path')

// all environments
app.set('port', process.env.TEST_PORT || 8080);
app.use(express.favicon());
app.use(express.logger('dev'));
app.use(express.bodyParser());
app.use(express.methodOverride());
app.use(express.static(path.join(__dirname,
'public')));

//Routes
```

```
app.get('/', function (req, res) {
  res.sendfile(__dirname + '/public/index.html');
});

app.get('/remote', function (req, res) {
  res.sendfile(__dirname + '/public/remote.html');
});

server.listen(app.get('port'), function(){
  console.log('Express server listening on port ' +
app.get('port'));
});
```

Above is the basic configuration of the Express HTTP server. For you to be able to test it, you should first create the static files, the remote.html and the index.html in the public directory. Write the "Hello, World" message into these pages and then execute them from the terminal:

```
node app.js
```

Or use:

```
npm start
```

For this to work, you must have added the following code snippet to the file Package.json:

```
...
"scripts": {
        "start": "node app.js"
    },
```

. . .

On the stdout of the server init, you will get the following:

```
Express server listening on port 8080
```

If you need to test the static pages, run your app in the background by use of & as shown below:

```
node app.js &
```

Our Node.js web server is now capable of serving the static files. We can launch our Chromium in the Kiosk mode, then test the web pages:

```
chromium --kiosk http://localhost:8080
```

Integrating Socket.io

For the purpose of providing real time connectivity on each browser, the Socket.io will choose the most capable transport during runtime, and the API will not be affected.

To integrate the Socket.io, you only have to add the code given below to the app.js file:

```
var express = require('express')
  , app = express()
  , server = require('http').createServer(app)
  , path = require('path')
  , io = require('socket.io').listen(server)
  , spawn = require('child_process').spawn
```

The logs can be minified by adding the following:

```
//Socket.io Config
io.set('log level', 1);
```

When using Socket.io for development, just know that you are developing a chat-like application.

The Socket.io server is now ready; but for now, it can do nothing. Let us implement the code that will process the messages and events sent from client to server.

The integration of Socket.io on the server side is as follows:

```
io.sockets.on('connection', function (socket) {
    socket.emit('message', { message: 'welcome to the
chat' });
    socket.on('send', function (data) {
        //Emit to all
        io.sockets.emit('message', data);
    });
});
```

The server should be emitting the message "message" after a connection to a new client. It will also wait for the event "send" so as to process data and emit it to all the clients that have been connected.

There are two types of clients in our case, that is, the rPi display (TV) and mobile web app (remote).

```
var ss;
//Socket.io Server
```

```
io.sockets.on('connection', function (socket) {

  socket.on("screen", function(data){
    socket.type = "screen";
    //Save the screen socket
    ss = socket;
    console.log("Screen ready...");
  });

  socket.on("remote", function(data){
    socket.type = "remote";
    console.log("Remote ready...");
    if(ss != undefined){
       console.log("Synced...");
    }
  });
)};
```

Implementing Client-Side Web Socket

Add the script given below to the file remote.html:

```
<script src="/socket.io/socket.io.js"> </script>
<script>
  //use http://raspberryPi.local if your using Avahi Service
    //or use your RasperryPi IP instead
    var socket = io.connect('http://raspberrypi.local:8080');
  socket.on('connect', function(data){
    socket.emit('screen');
  });
</script>
```

The following script should then be added to index.html:

```
<script src="/socket.io/socket.io.js"> </script>
<script>
  //use http://raspberryPi.local if your using Avahi Service
    //or use your RasperryPi IP instead
```

```
    var socket = io.connect('http://raspberrypi.local:8080');
  socket.on('connect', function(data){
    socket.emit('screen');
  });
</script>
```

With Node.js, we are able to run system commands in the given privileges of the child process. You can also pass arguments to commands, and performing piping of output from commands.

The Node.js commands can be executed as follows from the Child process:

```
spawn('echo',['foobar']);
```

If you are in need of piping the response to some other call, the callback function given below should be provided to the function:

```
//Run then pipe the shell script output
function run_shell(cmd, args, cb, end) {
    var spawn = require('child_process').spawn,
        child = spawn(cmd, args),
        me = this;
    child.stdout.on('data', function (buffer) { cb(me, buffer) });
    child.stdout.on('end', end);
}
```

Adding OMXControl

With the OMXControl module, you are able to control the OMX-Player via HTTP. The following will be needed in the main file for the project:

```
var omx = require('omxcontrol');

//use it with express
app.use(omx());
```

The OMXControl module will create the routes given below for the purpose of controlling the video playback:

```
http://localhost:8080/omx/start/:filename
http://localhost:8080/omx/pause
http://localhost:8080/omx/quit
```

The complete app.js file should be as follows:

```
var express = require('express')
  , app = express()
  , server = require('http').createServer(app)
  , path = require('path')
  , io = require('socket.io').listen(server)
  , spawn = require('child_process').spawn
  , omx = require('omxcontrol');

app.set('port', process.env.TEST_PORT || 8080);
app.use(express.favicon());
app.use(express.logger('dev'));
app.use(express.bodyParser());
app.use(express.methodOverride());
app.use(express.static(path.join(__dirname, 'public')));
app.use(omx());

app.get('/', function (req, res) {
  res.sendfile(__dirname + '/public/index.html');
});

app.get('/remote', function (req, res) {
  res.sendfile(__dirname + '/public/remote.html');
});

io.set('log level', 1);

server.listen(app.get('port'), function(){
  console.log('Express server listening on port ' + app.get('port'));
```

```
});

function run_shell(cmd, args, cb, end) {
    var spawn = require('child_process').spawn,
        child = spawn(cmd, args),
        me = this;
    child.stdout.on('data', function (buffer) { cb(me, buffer) });
    child.stdout.on('end', end);
}

var ss;
io.sockets.on('connection', function (socket) {

 socket.on("screen", function(data){
   socket.type = "screen";
   ss = socket;
   console.log("Screen ready...");
 });
 socket.on("remote", function(data){
   socket.type = "remote";
   console.log("Remote ready...");
 });

 socket.on("controll", function(data){
    console.log(data);
   if(socket.type === "remote"){

     if(data.action === "tap"){
        if(ss != undefined){
           ss.emit("controlling", {action:"enter"});
          }
      }
     else if(data.action === "swipeLeft"){
      if(ss != undefined){
         ss.emit("controlling", {action:"goLeft"});
          }
      }
     else if(data.action === "swipeRight"){
       if(ss != undefined){
          ss.emit("controlling", {action:"goRight"});
          }
     }
   }
 });

 socket.on("video", function(data){

    if( data.action === "play"){
    var id = data.video_id,
        url = "http://www.youtube.com/watch?v="+id;
```

65

```
    var runShell = new run_shell('youtube-dl',['-o','%(id)s.%(ext)s','-
f','/18/22',url],
        function (me, buffer) {
            me.stdout += buffer.toString();
            socket.emit("loading",{output: me.stdout});
            console.log(me.stdout)
        },
        function () {
            //child = spawn('omxplayer',[id+'.mp4']);
            omx.start(id+'.mp4');
        });
    }

});
});
```

Client Side Scripting

We can now begin to script on the client side.

Dashboard and Remote Mobile-app

We will not discuss how to create the front-end of the app. Instead of having to create a remote made up of buttons, we can choose to use the Quo.js. This is a nice cross-platform swipe gestures library for JavaScript.

```
$$(".r-container").swipeLeft(function(){
socket.emit('control',{action:"swipeLeft"});
});
```

For me to send the "Control" message back to the server with "swipeLeft" as the data action, I can use the approach given below. The server will send the message to the screen, and the screen client will selected square to next app.

66

The following should be added to the between the
<head></head> tags in the HTML:

```
<link rel="apple-touch-icon" href="images/custom_icon.png"/>
<link rel="apple-touch-startup-image" href="images/startup.png">
<meta name="viewport" content="width=device-width initial-scale=1, maximum-scale=1, user-scalable=no" />
<meta name="apple-mobile-web-app-title" content="Remote">
<meta name="apple-mobile-web-app-capable" content="yes">
```

67

Chapter 8- Installing Kodi on Raspberry Pi 3

The easiest way to have cheap XBMC, HD streamer is by installing Kodi on your Raspberry Pi 3. Kodi is one of the best of the streaming software that can help you create a speedy and dedicated media dongle. You should have the Raspberry Pi 3, Linux distribution and a few cables. Assemble the components, then follow the steps given below:

Installing Kodi

To use the Raspberry Pi as a media center, use any of the available purpose-built OSes and these will help you get started. I prefer using OSMC, which is a version of Kodi readily optimized to be used in the Pi device.

If you are not familiar with microSD card flashing, Linux distros and disk images, it is advisable that you use the Raspbmc, a default OS option that comes with NOOBS installer for Raspberry Pi Foundation. To use this, follow the normal guidelines for setting up the Raspberry Pi, then choose Raspbmc as the distro package to install other than the Raspbian.

Wi-Fi Setup

After installation and boot up, you should setup the Wi-Fi.

Open the Programs tab, then the Raspbmc settings menu. You will be allowed to enter the details for your Wi-Fi network such as the name and password. After, you will be connected to the Wi-Fi.

Adding the Remote Control

At this point, we should add a remote control to the Raspberry Pi. You don't need to control it with a keyboard and mouse as this is tiresome. If your TV is capable of supporting HDMI CEC,you are lucky as the standard TV remote will be compatible with the Pi. You will then be able to browse the content while seated on your coach.

It is also possible for you to control this via a web interface. You only have to go to the Raspbmc's system info menu, note down the IP address of the Raspberry Pi, then type the address into the browser. However, since you are using it from the browser, you will have to use the http:// prefix and the two computers should be on the same network. After the web UI has been opened, choose the "remote" tab, and a control interface will be provided that you can use to navigate to the contents.

For smartphone and tablet users, it is also possible for you to control the Pi from the device.

Playing the Files

Now that everything has been setup, we can go to the most important part, which is watching TV and movies. This is straight forward. Just plug in the flash drive or an external hard drive having the media in it. The Raspberry Pi will detect this automatically.

You can open the necessary tab, whether music, movies or video, then choose your storage device. You will see the files ready for playing. If you have a NAS drive, the Raspbmc is able to read and play the files from there, but the use of a thumb drive is the simplest way of doing it.

Setting up AirPlay

If you are a fan of Apple with a lot of content from iTunes, it is also possible for you to setup the Raspberry Pi as an AirPlay receiver. Open the AirPlay tab from the services tab, then tick the "allow XBMC to receive AirPlay content" option. Once you are done, the Apple device will detect the Raspberry Pi as an AirPlay Receiver, and you will be in a position to see all the contents from the iTunes store.

After doing all the above, you can start to stream your content in HD. It will be a nice experience as the Raspbmc is updated on a constant basis, and it provides a number of add-ons and options that can be altered to give you the kind of experience you need.

Chapter 9- Face Detection in Raspberry Pi

In this project, we will use the OpenCV to detect faces in the Raspberry Pi 3. To detect objects by use of cascade files, you should first get the cascade files.

The following components are needed for this project:

- Raspberry Pi 3 Model B

- Raspberry Pi Camera Module

You should also already have your Pi installed with Raspbian OS. You need to have installed PuTTY, an open source software for telnet and SSH client. We will be using the PuTTY software to access our Raspberry Pi remotely.

Your machine should also be installed with Open Source Computer Vision Library (OpenCV). This computer vision software can be used for machine learning. The software was developed to help provide a common infrastructure for the computer vision applications and for acceleration of the use of machine learning perception in commercial products. The OpenCV can easily be used in business, and it is easy for to customize the code. The library has over 2500 optimized algorithms that can be used for recognition of faces, identification of objects, tracking camera movements, classifying human actions in videos and extracting D models for objects.

You should first install the OpenCV into your computer. The

steps for doing this have already being discussed in previous chapters, so consult them.

Enabling the Camera

For the purpose of face recognition, you have to configure and enable the camera. To enable the camera, run the following command:

```
Sudo raspi-config
```

A small window will pop up with a number of options from which you can choose the one you want. Choose the option that says "Enable/Disable connection to the Raspberry Pi Camera". The password for the default user needs to be changed, so ensure you have done this for your camera. Set the interfacing options for the camera module. Lastly, you will be asked whether you need the camera module to be enabled, so choose "Yes". You will get a notification that your camera module has been enabled.

To test if this was successful, you just have to take a picture to know whether it is working correctly.

Chapter 10- Raspberry Pi Print Server

In this chapter, we will help you learn how to setup a print server in the Raspberry Pi. Installation of the software is somewhat easy, but much work is needed to configure it and make the Windows network find the print server. After that, you will have your printer setup, and this can be moved to any location and be accessible to multiple computers.

This will be done by use of software named CUPS (Common Unix Printing System). It forms the backbone of most printing software in Linux. It is the one responsible for communicating with the printer and getting printing work done. The following components are needed for this chapter:

- Raspberry Pi 3
- Micro SD Card
- Ethernet Cord or Wi-Fi dongle (Pi 3 has its Wi-Fi inbuilt)
- USB Printer

Optional:

- Raspberry Pi Case
- USB Keyboard
- USB Mouse

<u>Installing the Print Server Software</u>

The software is available through Debian Jessie packages. First, update the Pi to ensure you are using the latest version of the software. Run the following commands on the terminal:

```
sudo apt-get update
sudo apt-get upgrade
```

After the Pi has been updated, we can begin to install the print software. This will be CUPS that can manage printers attached through a USB or via the network. Run the following command on the terminal:

```
sudo apt-get install cups
```

After the installation of the software is complete, you will be required to perform a number of configurations. The Pi user should be added to lpadmin group. With this, the Pi user will be in a position to access the administrative functions for CUPS with no need for the super user. The user can be added to the group by running the following command:

```
sudo usermod -a -G lpadmin pi
```

For CUPS to be accessible throughout the network, we have to configure this. With the current setting, any non-localhost traffic will be blocked. To make it accept all traffic, we must run the following command:

```
sudo cupsctl --remote-any
sudo /etc/init.d/cups restart
```

At this point, we should be able to access the print server from any computer located on the network. If you don't know the IP address of your Pi, then run the following command:

```
hostname -I
```

Once you are aware of the IP address, use it on the browser as shown below:

```
http://192.168.1.105:631
```

SAMBA also needs to be setup correctly so that Windows can identify the print server correctly. The next section helps you set this up.

Set up SAMBA

For you to be in a position to use the print server with Windows in the correct way, you will have to set up SAMBA. We will install and configure it so that it can use the CUPS print drivers correctly.
Run the following command on the terminal:

```
sudo apt-get install samba
```

The command will help you install SAMBA. Let's open its file to make the necessary configuration changes:

```
sudo nano /etc/samba/smb.conf
```

Press Ctrl + V to move to the bottom of the file. Now that you are at the bottom of the file, you can add the following section; but if it is there, you will only have to change it to match the following;

```
# CUPS printing.
[printers]
comment = All Printers
browseable = no
path = /var/spool/samba
printable = yes
guest ok = yes
read only = yes
create mask = 0700

# Windows clients will look for this share name as a
source of the downloadable
# printer drivers
[print$]
comment = Printer Drivers
path = /var/lib/samba/printers
browseable = yes
read only = no
guest ok = no
```

Hit Ctrl + to save the file so as to exit. We can then restart SAMBA for the changes to take effect. The following command will help us do this:

```
sudo /etc/init.d/samba restart
```

Add the Printer to CUPS

This can be done easily, but we should first load the web interface for CUPS. If you are not sure of the IP address for the Pi, run the following command on the terminal;

```
hostname -I
```

Now that you are aware of the IP address of your Pi, open the browser, then type the following address:

```
https://192.168.1.105:631
```

Make sure you replace the above IP address with the one for your Pi. In the web interface opened, click on "Administration". Once the Administration window is open, click on "Add Printer".

A new window will pop up from which you will be able to choose the printer you need. Choose that printer, then click on "Continue". Your printer may not show up on the screen. To solve this, ensure that your printer is connected to one of the Pi's ports and that it is turned on. It will show automatically. If the problem persists, restart the Pi.

You can then choose the model for your printer. CUPS is capable of detecting this automatically and choosing the right driver. However, if this fails to work, you will have to browse through the list, then choose the right driver. Once everything is setup correctly, click the "Add Printer" button.

Next, set the name and description you need. You can also set the location in case you have multiple printers and need to work with them.

The option "Share This Printer" should be enabled to ensure

that the other computers in the network can access the printer. Once done, click "Continue". You will be presented with a new screen that will allow you to change some aspects of the printer. These include the print quality, the page's print size as well as other options. After this, we will add the newly set print server to Windows.

Adding the Print Server to Windows

For you to add the CUPS printer to Windows, a lot of work may have to be done as you will be expected to choose the necessary drivers for the connection to be successful.

To start, open the Windows network page by loading up "This PC" or "My Computer". You will then click on "network" from the sidebar.

Double click on your Pi and you will be asked for the username and password. Press enter, and if it fails to work, type in pi as the username. A window showing you all the printers available in your Pi will be presented. Identify the printer you need to connect to and double click it. You may see a warning message, but simply click "OK" to continue.

A connection with the printer will then be loaded up. If you need to make it the default printer for your computer, click on Printer, then "Set as Default Printer". The printer will be made available for use by any program and it will have been added to the computer successfully. You can then test the printer by trying to print a file.

You may experience some problems when trying to print. In such a case, it will be good for you to ensure that you have selected the right printer driver in both Windows and CUPS. You also need to ensure that your printer is on. Some printers will not turn on automatically once a file has been sent to it for printing. You can then enjoy printing. Congratulations!

Chapter 11- Setting up a Weather Station

In this chapter, we will show you how to use Sense HAT and Raspberry Pi 3 to set up a weather station. You will then be able to use this station to monitor the weather from your room or from anywhere.

The Sense HAT is equipment with numerous sensors contained in a single package. It provides you with an easy-to-add sensor to your Pi without extra circuitry. It has three primary sensors, and we will use them to detect humidity, temperature and pressure. The code is written in Python.

Begin by assembling the following components:

- Raspberry Pi 3

- Sense HAT

- Micro SD Card

- Raspberry Pi Case (optional)

Before beginning, first place the Sense HAT in the correct GPIO pins. Then update the Pi to ensure it is running the latest software version:

```
sudo apt-get update
sudo apt-get upgrade
```

We can then install the Sense Hat software package which will provide us with all libraries necessary to interact with the Sense HAT. After installation, a reboot will be necessary for the new software to begin working effectively:

```
sudo apt-get install sense-hat
sudo reboot
```

Let us create the file for the script by running the following command;

```
sudo nano ~/sensehat_test.py
```

Add the following line to the file:

```
from sense_hat import SenseHat
```

The purpose of the above line is to import the Sense Hat module from the sense_hat library. Add the following line:

```
sense = SenseHat()
```

The above line will help establish a link to the Sense Hat library and initialize it for us to begin making calls to it. Add the next line given below to the script:

```
sense.show_message("Hello World")
```

The above line should write the message, "Hello World", so

you should see the message scroll across RGB lights.

Press Ctrl + X, then hit Y plus enter to exit the file. You will have saved the file, so run it by executing the following command from the terminal:

```
sudo python ~/sensehat_test.py
```

You should see the "Hello World" message scrolling.

We can now begin to write the script for the weather station. Create the script file by running the following command on the terminal:

```
sudo nano ~/weather_script.py
```

Add the following lines to the script:

```
#!/usr/bin/python
from sense_hat import SenseHat
import time
import sys
```

The above lines help us import the libraries needed. Add the following code to the script, so that you end up with the following in your file:

```
#!/usr/bin/python
from sense_hat import SenseHat
import time
import sys

sense = SenseHat()
sense.clear()
```

```
try:
    while True:
        temp = sense.get_temperature()
        temp = round(temp, 1)
        print("Temperature C",temp)

        humidity = sense.get_humidity()
        humidity = round(humidity, 1)
        print("Humidity :",humidity)

        pressure = sense.get_pressure()
        pressure = round(pressure, 1)
        print("Pressure:",pressure)

        time.sleep(1)
except KeyboardInterrupt:
    pass
```

A link to the sense hat library has been created, The LED matrix has been cleared, so you will see all the LEDs go off. The indentation for the "while" should be maintained. The line:

```
temp = sense.get_temperature()
```

helps us retrieve the temperature by calling the sensor. The output will be in Celsius. If you need to convert it to Fahrenheit, use the following line:

```
temp = 1.8 * round(temp, 1)  + 32
```

The pressure and humidity sensors have been read in the same way to that of temperature.

Save and exit the code by pressing Ctrl + X, then Y, and hit enter. Run the script by typing the following command on the terminal:

```
sudo python ~/weather_script.py
```

The values for temperature, humidity and pressure will be shown. To stop your script from running, just hit ctrl + c.

Using LED Matrix

We now need to perform an improvement to our weather station. We will change it so that the results can be displayed on the LED matrix. Open the script by running the following command:

```
sudo nano ~/weather_script.py
```

Add the line given below just above the "time.sleep(1);" line:

```
sense.show_message("Temperature C" + str(temp) + "Humidity:" + str(humidity) +
"Pressure:" + str(pressure), scroll_speed=(0.08), back_colour= [0,0,200])
```

Ensure that all of the above code has been typed in a single line. The line will make the values for temperature, pressure and humidity scroll across the LED Matrix of Sense Hat.
We also need to ensure that the LED Matrix has been cleared once the script is killed for any reason. Add the following line at the script's bottom and after exception handling:

```
sense.clear()
```

Once the above changes have been made, you should end up with the following script:

```
#!/usr/bin/python
from sense_hat import SenseHat
import time
import sys

sense = SenseHat()
sense.clear()

try:
    while True:
        temp = sense.get_temperature()
        temp = round(temp, 1)
        print("Temperature C",temp)

        humidity = sense.get_humidity()
        humidity = round(humidity, 1)
        print("Humidity :",humidity)

        pressure = sense.get_pressure()
        pressure = round(pressure, 1)
        print("Pressure:",pressure)

        sense.show_message("Temperature C" + str(temp) \
            + "Humidity:" + str(humidity) + "Pressure:" \
            + str(pressure), scroll_speed=(0.08), back_colour= [0,0,200])

        time.sleep(1)
except KeyboardInterrupt:
    pass

sense.clear()
```

You can then press Ctrl + X, then Y, and hit the enter key. You will have saved and exited the script. Let us run it to test whether it is operating as expected by running the following command on the command prompt:

```
sudo python ~/weather_script.py
```

You will see the text begin to scroll across the LED matrix of the Sense Hat.

Using Initial State

Initial State is simply a website designed to be used for data storage as well as data analytics for IoT (Internet of things) devices like the Raspberry Pi. Open the website and sign up.

You just have to open the website, click on SIGN IN, then choose "Register A New Account".

Sign in to get an API key. Once the home page is open, look beneath "Streaming Access Keys" and find the "Create a New Key" button. Click the button and save the key.

We can then get the Python streamer for Initial State. The install script can be obtained directly from their website. The code can be viewed by opening the https://get.initialstate.com/python url on the browser. To enter, the script, run the following command on the terminal:

```
curl -sSL https://get.initialstate.com/python -o - |
sudo bash
```

A prompt will be presented to you. Hit the N key to skip. Now that the streamer has been download, we can begin to edit the previous script. Open the script by running the following command on the terminal:

```
sudo nano ~/weather_script.py
```

A number of codes will have to be added to the script. Add the line given below to the file:

```
import sys
```

Followed by the following line:
```
from ISStreamer.Streamer import Streamer
```

What we have done is imported the Initial State streamer package. This will allow us to establish a connection to the website then stream our data to it. Add the following line:

```
logger = Streamer(bucket_name="Sense Hat Sensor Data",
access_key="YOUR_KEY_HERE")
```

Below the following line:

```
sense = SenseHat()
```

We will have created the streamer. Replace the:

```
print(
```

With the following:

```
logger.log(
```

At this point, your code should be as follows:

```
#!/usr/bin/python
from sense_hat import SenseHat
import time
import sys
from ISStreamer.Streamer import Streamer
```

```
sense = SenseHat()
logger = Streamer(bucket_name="Sense Hat Sensor Data", access_key="YOUR_KEY_HERE")
sense.clear()

try:
    while True:
        temp = sense.get_temperature()
        temp = round(temp, 1)
        logger.log("Temperature C",temp)

        humidity = sense.get_humidity()
        humidity = round(humidity, 1)
        logger.log("Humidity :",humidity)

        pressure = sense.get_pressure()
        pressure = round(pressure, 1)
        logger.log("Pressure:",pressure)

        time.sleep(1)
except KeyboardInterrupt:
    pass
```

Save the script and exit the editor. Run the following command on the terminal:

```
sudo python ~/weather_script.py
```

Data will be send to the website immediately. This can be seen on the left-hand side of the website page.

Conclusion

We have come to the end of this guide. You should now be able to implement projects in your Raspberry Pi 3 on your own.

You must have known how useful the Raspberry Pi is. The device can have different uses including home automation. For instance, you can use the raspberry Pi for home security. The Pi can be programmed using different programming languages. Examples include Python and Node.JS. With such programming languages, one can create complex and useful apps using the Pi. For beginners in computer programming, the Raspberry Pi is the best device to begin with. Other than computer programming, one can learn the basics of computer science with the device.

Thank you!

Thank you for buying this book. If you enjoyed reading this text and developing all the fun projects, then I'd like to ask you for a favor. **Would you be kind enough to leave a review on Amazon?**
It'd be greatly appreciated!

All my best wishes,

Steve

Made in the USA
Lexington, KY
14 February 2018